BABY
JOURNAL BOOK

Baby's Daily Log

Date	Time	Minutes (Breastfeeding)	Ounces (Bottles)	Sleep / Wake	Wet	Poop
		R				
		L				
		R				
		L				
		L				
		R				
		L				
		R				
		L				
		R				
		L				
		R				
		L				
		R				
		L				
		R				
		L				
		R				
		L				

Baby's Daily Log

Date	Time	Minutes (Breastfeeding)	Ounces (Bottles)	Sleep Wake	Wet	Poop
		R				
		L				
		R				
		L				
		L				
		R				
		L				
		R				
		L				
		R				
		L				
		R				
		L				
		R				
		L				
		R				
		L				
		R				
		L				

Baby's Daily Log

Date	Time	Minutes (Breastfeeding)	Ounces (Bottles)	Sleep / Wake	Wet	Poop
		R				
		L				
		R				
		L				
		L				
		R				
		L				
		R				
		L				
		R				
		L				
		R				
		L				
		R				
		L				
		R				
		L				
		R				
		L				

Baby's Daily Log

Date	Time	Minutes (Breastfeeding)	Ounces (Bottles)	Sleep Wake	Wet	Poop
		R				
		L				
		R				
		L				
		L				
		R				
		L				
		R				
		L				
		R				
		L				
		R				
		L				
		R				
		L				
		R				
		L				
		R				
		L				

Baby's Daily Log

Date	Time	Minutes (Breastfeeding)	Ounces (Bottles)	Sleep / Wake	Wet	Poop
		R				
		L				
		R				
		L				
		L				
		R				
		L				
		R				
		L				
		R				
		L				
		R				
		L				
		R				
		L				
		R				
		L				
		R				
		L				

Baby's Daily Log

Date	Time	Minutes (Breastfeeding)	Ounces (Bottles)	Sleep / Wake	Wet	Poop
		R				
		L				
		R				
		L				
		L				
		R				
		L				
		R				
		L				
		R				
		L				
		R				
		L				
		R				
		L				
		R				
		L				
		R				
		L				

Baby's Daily Log

Date	Time	Minutes (Breastfeeding)	Ounces (Bottles)	Sleep Wake	Wet	Poop
		R				
		L				
		R				
		L				
		L				
		R				
		L				
		R				
		L				
		R				
		L				
		R				
		L				
		R				
		L				
		R				
		L				
		R				
		L				

Baby's Daily Log

Date	Time	Minutes (Breastfeeding)	Ounces (Bottles)	Sleep / Wake	Wet	Poop
		R				
		L				
		R				
		L				
		L				
		R				
		L				
		R				
		L				
		R				
		L				
		R				
		L				
		R				
		L				
		R				
		L				
		R				
		L				

Baby's Daily Log

Date	Time	Minutes (Breastfeeding)	Ounces (Bottles)	Sleep Wake	Wet	Poop
		R				
		L				
		R				
		L				
		L				
		R				
		L				
		R				
		L				
		R				
		L				
		R				
		L				
		R				
		L				
		R				
		L				
		R				
		L				

Baby's Daily Log

Date	Time	Minutes (Breastfeeding)	Ounces (Bottles)	Sleep / Wake	Wet	Poop
		R				
		L				
		R				
		L				
		L				
		R				
		L				
		R				
		L				
		R				
		L				
		R				
		L				
		R				
		L				
		R				
		L				
		R				
		L				

Baby's Daily Log

Date	Time	Minutes (Breastfeeding)	Ounces (Bottles)	Sleep	Wet	Poop
				Wake		
		R				
		L				
		R				
		L				
		L				
		R				
		L				
		R				
		L				
		R				
		L				
		R				
		L				
		R				
		L				
		R				
		L				
		R				
		L				

Baby's Daily Log

Date	Time	Minutes (Breastfeeding)	Ounces (Bottles)	Sleep Wake	Wet	Poop
		R				
		L				
		R				
		L				
		L				
		R				
		L				
		R				
		L				
		R				
		L				
		R				
		L				
		R				
		L				
		R				
		L				
		R				
		L				

Baby's Daily Log

Date	Time	Minutes (Breastfeeding)	Ounces (Bottles)	Sleep / Wake	Wet	Poop
		R				
		L				
		R				
		L				
		L				
		R				
		L				
		R				
		L				
		R				
		L				
		R				
		L				
		R				
		L				
		R				
		L				
		R				
		L				

Baby's Daily Log

Date	Time	Minutes (Breastfeeding)	Ounces (Bottles)	Sleep / Wake	Wet	Poop
		R				
		L				
		R				
		L				
		L				
		R				
		L				
		R				
		L				
		R				
		L				
		R				
		L				
		R				
		L				
		R				
		L				
		R				
		L				

Baby's Daily Log

Date	Time	Minutes (Breastfeeding)	Ounces (Bottles)	Sleep / Wake	Wet	Poop
		R				
		L				
		R				
		L				
		L				
		R				
		L				
		R				
		L				
		R				
		L				
		R				
		L				
		R				
		L				
		R				
		L				
		R				
		L				

Baby's Daily Log

Date	Time	Minutes (Breastfeeding)	Ounces (Bottles)	Sleep / Wake	Wet	Poop
		R				
		L				
		R				
		L				
		L				
		R				
		L				
		R				
		L				
		R				
		L				
		R				
		L				
		R				
		L				
		R				
		L				
		R				
		L				

Baby's Daily Log

Date	Time	Minutes (Breastfeeding)	Ounces (Bottles)	Sleep	Wet	Poop
				Wake		
		R				
		L				
		R				
		L				
		L				
		R				
		L				
		R				
		L				
		R				
		L				
		R				
		L				
		R				
		L				
		R				
		L				
		R				
		L				

Baby's Daily Log

Date	Time	Minutes (Breastfeeding)	Ounces (Bottles)	Sleep Wake	Wet	Poop
		R				
		L				
		R				
		L				
		L				
		R				
		L				
		R				
		L				
		R				
		L				
		R				
		L				
		R				
		L				
		R				
		L				
		R				
		L				

Baby's Daily Log

Date	Time	Minutes (Breastfeeding)	Ounces (Bottles)	Sleep / Wake	Wet	Poop
		R				
		L				
		R				
		L				
		L				
		R				
		L				
		R				
		L				
		R				
		L				
		R				
		L				
		R				
		L				
		R				
		L				
		R				
		L				

Baby's Daily Log

Date	Time	Minutes (Breastfeeding)	Ounces (Bottles)	Sleep Wake	Wet	Poop
		R				
		L				
		R				
		L				
		L				
		R				
		L				
		R				
		L				
		R				
		L				
		R				
		L				
		R				
		L				
		R				
		L				
		R				
		L				

Baby's Daily Log

Date	Time	Minutes (Breastfeeding)	Ounces (Bottles)	Sleep Wake	Wet	Poop
		R				
		L				
		R				
		L				
		L				
		R				
		L				
		R				
		L				
		R				
		L				
		R				
		L				
		R				
		L				
		R				
		L				
		R				
		L				

Baby's Daily Log

Date	Time	Minutes (Breastfeeding)	Ounces (Bottles)	Sleep Wake	Wet	Poop
		R				
		L				
		R				
		L				
		L				
		R				
		L				
		R				
		L				
		R				
		L				
		R				
		L				
		R				
		L				
		R				
		L				
		R				
		L				

Baby's Daily Log

Date	**Time**	**Minutes** (Breastfeeding)	**Ounces** (Bottles)	**Sleep** **Wake**	**Wet**	**Poop**
		R				
		L				
		R				
		L				
		L				
		R				
		L				
		R				
		L				
		R				
		L				
		R				
		L				
		R				
		L				
		R				
		L				
		R				
		L				

Baby's Daily Log

Date	Time	Minutes (Breastfeeding)	Ounces (Bottles)	Sleep Wake	Wet	Poop
		R				
		L				
		R				
		L				
		L				
		R				
		L				
		R				
		L				
		R				
		L				
		R				
		L				
		R				
		L				
		R				
		L				
		R				
		L				

Baby's Daily Log

Date	Time	Minutes (Breastfeeding)	Ounces (Bottles)	Sleep / Wake	Wet	Poop
		R				
		L				
		R				
		L				
		L				
		R				
		L				
		R				
		L				
		R				
		L				
		R				
		L				
		R				
		L				
		R				
		L				
		R				
		L				

Baby's Daily Log

Date	Time	Minutes (Breastfeeding)	Ounces (Bottles)	Sleep	Wet	Poop
				Wake		
		R				
		L				
		R				
		L				
		L				
		R				
		L				
		R				
		L				
		R				
		L				
		R				
		L				
		R				
		L				
		R				
		L				
		R				
		L				

Baby's Daily Log

Date	Time	Minutes (Breastfeeding)	Ounces (Bottles)	Sleep Wake	Wet	Poop
		R				
		L				
		R				
		L				
		L				
		R				
		L				
		R				
		L				
		R				
		L				
		R				
		L				
		R				
		L				
		R				
		L				
		R				
		L				

Baby's Daily Log

Date	Time	Minutes (Breastfeeding)	Ounces (Bottles)	Sleep Wake	Wet	Poop
		R				
		L				
		R				
		L				
		L				
		R				
		L				
		R				
		L				
		R				
		L				
		R				
		L				
		R				
		L				
		R				
		L				
		R				
		L				

Baby's Daily Log

Date	Time	Minutes (Breastfeeding)	Ounces (Bottles)	Sleep / Wake	Wet	Poop
		R				
		L				
		R				
		L				
		L				
		R				
		L				
		R				
		L				
		R				
		L				
		R				
		L				
		R				
		L				
		R				
		L				
		R				
		L				

Baby's Daily Log

Date	Time	Minutes (Breastfeeding)	Ounces (Bottles)	Sleep / Wake	Wet	Poop
		R				
		L				
		R				
		L				
		L				
		R				
		L				
		R				
		L				
		R				
		L				
		R				
		L				
		R				
		L				
		R				
		L				
		R				
		L				

Baby's Daily Log

Date	Time	Minutes (Breastfeeding)	Ounces (Bottles)	Sleep	Wet	Poop
				Wake		
		R				
		L				
		R				
		L				
		L				
		R				
		L				
		R				
		L				
		R				
		L				
		R				
		L				
		R				
		L				
		R				
		L				
		R				
		L				

Baby's Daily Log

Date	Time	Minutes (Breastfeeding)	Ounces (Bottles)	Sleep / Wake	Wet	Poop
		R				
		L				
		R				
		L				
		L				
		R				
		L				
		R				
		L				
		R				
		L				
		R				
		L				
		R				
		L				
		R				
		L				
		R				
		L				

Baby's Daily Log

Date	Time	Minutes (Breastfeeding)	Ounces (Bottles)	Sleep / Wake	Wet	Poop
		R				
		L				
		R				
		L				
		L				
		R				
		L				
		R				
		L				
		R				
		L				
		R				
		L				
		R				
		L				
		R				
		L				
		R				
		L				

Baby's Daily Log

Date	Time	Minutes (Breastfeeding)	Ounces (Bottles)	Sleep Wake	Wet	Poop
		R				
		L				
		R				
		L				
		L				
		R				
		L				
		R				
		L				
		R				
		L				
		R				
		L				
		R				
		L				
		R				
		L				
		R				
		L				

Baby's Daily Log

Date	Time	Minutes (Breastfeeding)	Ounces (Bottles)	Sleep Wake	Wet	Poop
		R				
		L				
		R				
		L				
		L				
		R				
		L				
		R				
		L				
		R				
		L				
		R				
		L				
		R				
		L				
		R				
		L				
		R				
		L				

Baby's Daily Log

Date	Time	Minutes (Breastfeeding)	Ounces (Bottles)	Sleep / Wake	Wet	Poop
		R				
		L				
		R				
		L				
		L				
		R				
		L				
		R				
		L				
		R				
		L				
		R				
		L				
		R				
		L				
		R				
		L				
		R				
		L				

Baby's Daily Log

Date	Time	Minutes (Breastfeeding)	Ounces (Bottles)	Sleep / Wake	Wet	Poop
		R				
		L				
		R				
		L				
		L				
		R				
		L				
		R				
		L				
		R				
		L				
		R				
		L				
		R				
		L				
		R				
		L				
		R				
		L				

Baby's Daily Log

Date	Time	Minutes (Breastfeeding)	Ounces (Bottles)	Sleep Wake	Wet	Poop
		R				
		L				
		R				
		L				
		L				
		R				
		L				
		R				
		L				
		R				
		L				
		R				
		L				
		R				
		L				
		R				
		L				
		R				
		L				

Baby's Daily Log

Date	Time	Minutes (Breastfeeding)	Ounces (Bottles)	Sleep	Wet	Poop
				Wake		
		R				
		L				
		R				
		L				
		L				
		R				
		L				
		R				
		L				
		R				
		L				
		R				
		L				
		R				
		L				
		R				
		L				
		R				
		L				

Baby's Daily Log

Date	Time	Minutes (Breastfeeding)	Ounces (Bottles)	Sleep	Wet	Poop
				Wake		
		R				
		L				
		R				
		L				
		L				
		R				
		L				
		R				
		L				
		R				
		L				
		R				
		L				
		R				
		L				
		R				
		L				
		R				
		L				

Baby's Daily Log

Date	Time	Minutes (Breastfeeding)	Ounces (Bottles)	Sleep / Wake	Wet	Poop
		R				
		L				
		R				
		L				
		L				
		R				
		L				
		R				
		L				
		R				
		L				
		R				
		L				
		R				
		L				
		R				
		L				
		R				
		L				

Baby's Daily Log

Date	Time	Minutes (Breastfeeding)	Ounces (Bottles)	Sleep / Wake	Wet	Poop
		R				
		L				
		R				
		L				
		L				
		R				
		L				
		R				
		L				
		R				
		L				
		R				
		L				
		R				
		L				
		R				
		L				
		R				
		L				

Baby's Daily Log

Date	Time	Minutes (Breastfeeding)	Ounces (Bottles)	Sleep / Wake	Wet	Poop
		R				
		L				
		R				
		L				
		L				
		R				
		L				
		R				
		L				
		R				
		L				
		R				
		L				
		R				
		L				
		R				
		L				
		R				
		L				

Baby's Daily Log

Date	Time	Minutes (Breastfeeding)	Ounces (Bottles)	Sleep / Wake	Wet	Poop
		R				
		L				
		R				
		L				
		L				
		R				
		L				
		R				
		L				
		R				
		L				
		R				
		L				
		R				
		L				
		R				
		L				
		R				
		L				

Baby's Daily Log

Date	Time	Minutes (Breastfeeding)	Ounces (Bottles)	Sleep / Wake	Wet	Poop
		R				
		L				
		R				
		L				
		L				
		R				
		L				
		R				
		L				
		R				
		L				
		R				
		L				
		R				
		L				
		R				
		L				
		R				
		L				

Baby's Daily Log

Date	Time	Minutes (Breastfeeding)	Ounces (Bottles)	Sleep	Wet	Poop
				Wake		
		R				
		L				
		R				
		L				
		L				
		R				
		L				
		R				
		L				
		R				
		L				
		R				
		L				
		R				
		L				
		R				
		L				
		R				
		L				

Baby's Daily Log

Date	Time	Minutes (Breastfeeding)	Ounces (Bottles)	Sleep	Wet	Poop
				Wake		
		R				
		L				
		R				
		L				
		L				
		R				
		L				
		R				
		L				
		R				
		L				
		R				
		L				
		R				
		L				
		R				
		L				
		R				
		L				

Baby's Daily Log

Date	Time	Minutes (Breastfeeding)	Ounces (Bottles)	Sleep Wake	Wet	Poop
		R				
		L				
		R				
		L				
		L				
		R				
		L				
		R				
		L				
		R				
		L				
		R				
		L				
		R				
		L				
		R				
		L				
		R				
		L				

CPSIA information can be obtained at www.ICGtesting.com
Printed in the USA
LVOW02s1456010915

452375LV00009B/230/P

9 781681 278162